*Cornerstones of Freedom*

# Hiroshima and Nagasaki

Barbara Silberdick Feinberg

CHILDRENS PRESS®
CHICAGO

**Library of Congress Cataloging-in-Publication Data**

Feinberg, Barbara Silberdick.
  Hiroshima and Nagasaki/ by Barbara Silberdick Feinberg.
    p.  cm.–(Cornerstones of freedom)
  ISBN 0-516-06627-7
  1. Hiroshima-shi (Japan)—History—Bombardment, 1945—
Juvenile literature. 2. Nagasaki-shi–(Japan)—History—
Bombardment, 1945—Juvenile literature.  I. Title.  II. Series.
D767.25.HGF45 1995
940.54'25—dc20                              95-2683
                                              CIP
                                               AC

©1995 by Childrens Press®, Inc.
All rights reserved. Published simultaneously in Canada.
Printed in the United States of America.
1 2 3 4 5 6 7 8 9 10 R 04 03 02 01 00 99 98 97 96 95

*Colonel Paul W. Tibbets with the* Enola Gay

At 2:45 in the morning, August 6, 1945, the *Enola Gay,* a B-29 bomber, took off on a secret mission from Tinian Island in the South Pacific. Its destination was Hiroshima, Japan, about 1,500 miles away. There was no guarantee that the mission would succeed. After all, no one had ever dropped an atomic bomb from a plane.

Paul W. Tibbets, commander of the 509th Composite Group, piloted the bomber. His air force unit had been specially selected and trained for this flight. Despite many practice drills, the takeoff was dangerous and difficult. The B-29 was 15,000 pounds overweight. It was loaded with a 9,700-pound atomic bomb

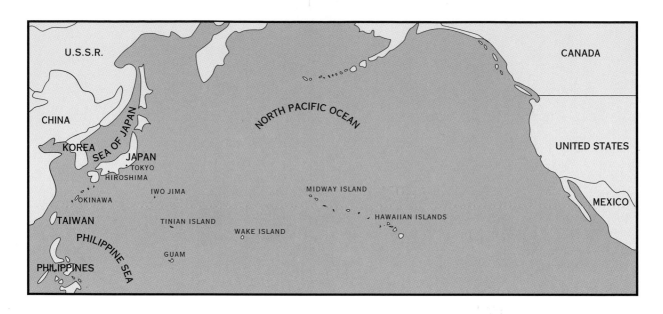

*To fight Japan in World War II, American forces traveled across the Pacific Ocean. To drop the atomic bomb on Japan, American planes took off from Tinian Island.*

*A replica of the "Little Boy" bomb*

nicknamed "Little Boy" and 7,000 gallons of fuel. The plane needed every inch of the two-mile runway to build up enough speed to become airborne. Aloft, the *Enola Gay* met with two other B-29s that carried cameras and instruments to measure the bomb's explosion.

Weapons expert Deke Parsons readied "Little Boy" to detonate once it left the plane. He constantly checked the green safety plugs that kept it from going off accidentally during the flight. To a member of the crew, the bomb resembled "an elongated ash can with fins." It was covered with signatures and messages from members of the American armed services. One read, "Greetings to the Emperor [of Japan] from the men of the *Indianapolis.*" The USS *Indianapolis* had carried "Little Boy" to Tinian on July 26. Three days later, the ship was sunk by a Japanese submarine in the Philippine Sea. More than 880 lives were lost.

At 7:30 A.M., the *Enola Gay* approached Hiroshima, Japan. Deke Parsons armed the bomb by removing the safety plugs. Timing devices would trigger the explosion after the bomb left the airplane. Copilot Robert Lewis later wrote in his diary of the moment when Parsons armed the bomb: "I had a feeling the bomb had a life of its own now."

Commander Tibbets reminded the crew to put on special goggles to shield their eyes from the intense light that would occur when the bomb went off. The men climbed into their "flak" suits, which protected them from possible antiaircraft fire. There was none. The people of Hiroshima were accustomed to seeing small groups of B-29s flying overhead to other destinations. They ignored the three B-29s and continued on their way to work or school.

*A photo of Hiroshima from the air, taken before the bomb was dropped*

As was customary on bombing runs, bombardier Major Thomas Ferebee took control of the *Enola Gay*. Looking through his bombsight, he piloted the plane toward the target. The Aioi Bridge in central Hiroshima was his aiming point. The Japanese Second Army Headquarters was nearby.

The bomb was released at 8:16 A.M., Hiroshima time. Forty-three seconds after it left the airplane, "Little Boy" detonated at 1,900 feet above the ground. It exploded with the force of 12,500 tons of TNT. Tibbets announced, "Fellows, you have just dropped the first atomic bomb in history." He had already turned the plane away from the city.

A shock wave hit the B-29 less than twelve miles away from Hiroshima. Navigator Theodore J. Van Kirk recalled, "The plane bounced, it jumped and there was a noise like a piece of sheet metal snapping." From the air, the crew saw a mushroom cloud of purple-gray smoke where the target had been. Electronics officer Jacob Beser wrote: "The city was burning for all she was worth. It looked like…well did you ever go to the beach and stir up sand in shallow water and see it all billow up? That's what it looked like to me." Lewis noted in his diary, "If I live a hundred years, I'll never quite get these few minutes out of my mind."

A mushroom cloud rose above Hiroshima after the atomic bomb was detonated. On the ground near the bomb's hypocenter, nearly every object and building were destroyed.

*Harry S. Truman*

News of the successful mission reached United States president Harry S. Truman on board the warship *Augusta*. He was returning to the United States from a meeting in Europe. Truman boasted to the ship's captain, "This is the greatest thing in history." He did not yet know how much destruction the bomb had caused.

Truman had become president after serving just three months as vice president under Franklin Delano Roosevelt. Roosevelt had died in office on April 12, 1945. He had guided the United States through most of World War II.

The war began on September 1, 1939, when Germany invaded Poland and then overpowered several other countries in Europe. Germany, Italy, and Japan became partners. They were known as the "Axis" powers and pledged to help one another. Germany and Italy battled European nations in Europe and in northern Africa. In the East, Japan waged war in China and eventually conquered much of Southeast Asia.

*Franklin Delano Roosevelt*

Japan's aggression in China angered the United States, and relations became strained between the two

*The Japanese surprise attack crippled the U.S. naval base at Pearl Harbor, Hawaii. Here, the USS Virginia billows fire and smoke.*

nations. Even while Japanese diplomats were in Washington, D.C., negotiating with the American government, Japan ordered a sneak attack on the United States. On December 7, 1941, without first declaring war, Japan carried out an air raid on the U.S. naval base at Pearl Harbor, Hawaii. The attack killed about 3,000 American servicemen, and destroyed and damaged a number of U.S. warships.

The American people were infuriated by the Japanese attack, and the United States entered World War II. Calling themselves the "Allies," the United States, Great Britain, China, the Soviet Union, and other countries fought against the Axis powers from 1942 to 1945.

Long before his death, President Roosevelt had been making plans to ensure an Allied victory in the war. He had never discussed these arrangements with Vice President Harry Truman. Only after Truman was sworn in as president in April 1945 did Secretary of War Henry Stimson tell him about the Manhattan Project. The Manhattan Project was the code name for the government's top-secret attempt to build an atomic bomb. It was given that name because much of the early research on the bomb was done in Manhattan (New York City).

American, British, and European scientists worked feverishly to develop the powerful, new weapon. They feared that Germany would complete its own bomb first. In 1944, however, U.S. intelligence agents discovered that Germany had abandoned its atomic bomb program at an early stage. Nevertheless, the Manhattan Project scientists continued their work.

*For several years, President Roosevelt (left) and Secretary of State Stimson (right) had overseen the secret Manhattan Project. The project's mission was to build an atomic bomb.*

In April 1945, Secretary Stimson told Truman that the bomb probably would be ready in about four months, at a cost of $2 billion. Meanwhile, on May 7, Germany surrendered to the Allies. Eager to end the war with Japan, the president had already decided to drop an atomic bomb on a Japanese city. He later wrote, "I regarded the bomb as a military weapon and never had any doubt that it should be used."

A Target Committee of scientists and military officers began surveying Japanese cities to pick possible targets for dropping the atomic bomb. They selected Yokohama, Hiroshima, Niigata, Kokura, and Kyoto. The committee turned in its report to Secretary Stimson at the end of May. Later, he removed Kyoto from the list. Kyoto was the ancient cultural center of Japanese life. Truman recorded in his diary, "Even if the Japs are savages, ruthless, merciless, and fanatic, we as the leader of the world...cannot drop this terrible bomb on the old capital." The city of Nagasaki was substituted for Kyoto.

Meanwhile, at Stimson's suggestion, Truman had formed the Interim Committee of government officials, assisted by scientists, to advise him on ways to use the bomb. On June 1, 1945, the president received the committee's recommendations: 1) The bomb should be exploded over a previously undamaged target to show the Japanese how powerful the new weapon was. 2) The Japanese should receive no prior warning that would enable them to move American prisoners of war to the target area. 3) No demonstration test should be held. The United States probably would have only two bombs by August, and both might not work.

Not everyone connected with the Manhattan Project agreed with the decision to drop the bomb. Some scientists condemned atomic bombing as immoral. Others insisted on a demonstration test to convince the Japanese to surrender. After the test, they wanted the government to negotiate an international agreement to control the development of atomic weapons. Otherwise, a costly and possibly destructive arms race would result. (For the next forty years, rival nations did develop atomic arsenals. Fear of mutual destruction kept the bombs from being used. In the late 1980s and 1990s, international agreements placed some limits on atomic weapons.)

Although some of the atomic bomb specialists opposed using the bomb, Truman never saw their statements. When their reports arrived, he was already on his way to Potsdam, Germany. There, he would meet with leaders of Britain and the Soviet Union to discuss the future of Europe and the defeat of Japan. The president had delayed his trip to Potsdam until July, when an atomic bomb would be ready for testing. If

*The three most powerful leaders of the Allies met at Potsdam in July 1945. Left to right: British prime minister Winston Churchill, U.S. president Harry Truman, and Soviet premier Joseph Stalin.*

the bomb worked, Truman planned to end the war by dropping the bomb on Japan. If the bomb did not work, Truman would have to persuade the Soviet Union to declare war on Japan. Relations between the United States and the Soviet Union already were strained.

At Potsdam, Soviet leader Joseph Stalin told Truman that the Japanese wanted to arrange a peace settlement. Having read American intelligence reports, the president was not surprised. He also knew that the Japanese were unwilling to accept the Allied surrender terms. Because of their sneak attack on Pearl Harbor, the president distrusted the Japanese. Stalin, too, was not ready to negotiate. The Soviet Union might reap more benefits by entering the war than by staying neutral.

On July 16, 1945, Truman's problems were solved when Manhattan Project scientists successfully exploded an atomic bomb in the New Mexican desert. Truman shared details of the bomb test with British prime minister Winston Churchill, but not with Joseph Stalin. The cautious president told the Soviet leader only that the United States had developed a powerful new weapon "of unusual destructive force." He did not identify or describe it. Stalin did not reveal what he knew, either. His spies at the Manhattan Project were keeping him informed of the latest developments. This helped the Soviets to later build their own atomic bomb. The predictions of some concerned American scientists had come true. The arms race had begun already.

*Manhattan Project technicians prepare the atomic bomb for testing at Alamogordo, New Mexico.*

*Thousands of personnel had been killed or injured at Okinawa, and in many other Pacific Ocean battles that occurred toward the end of the war.*

Truman was convinced that using the bomb would shorten the war and save lives. So far, the struggle to recapture Pacific islands from the Japanese had resulted in a bloodbath. In March 1945, about 6,000 Americans and 20,000 Japanese had been killed at Iwo Jima. More than 12,000 American and 110,000 Japanese died in the fighting on Okinawa in June. By mid-June, American planes had firebombed Tokyo and Japan's five largest industrial cities. At least 260,000 people were killed, 2 million buildings were destroyed, and some 13 million civilians were left homeless. Despite these terrible losses, the Japanese were still determined to fight. American military advisors told Truman that another million lives would be lost if they invaded the Japanese home islands.

On July 24, Truman ordered the Air Force to drop atomic bombs on Japan between August 3 and August 10 unless Japan surrendered. Then, on July 26, the Potsdam Declaration was issued by the Allies. Without mentioning the atomic bomb, it gave the Japanese a choice between "unconditional surrender" or "prompt and utter destruction."

The choice was unacceptable to the Japanese. Unconditional surrender would destroy their way of life. They did not want to dissolve their government, dethrone their emperor, or be occupied and ruled by a foreign nation. Truman stood firm. "It occurred to me that a quarter of a million of the [best] of our young manhood were worth a couple of Japanese cities...."

One of those cities was Hiroshima. On August 6, 1945, it was destroyed in an instant when the *Enola Gay* dropped its bomb. The bomb's hypocenter (the spot directly below its detonation) was 500 feet away from the Aioi Bridge, at Shima Hospital. People caught within a half-mile of the hypocenter were immediately reduced to black char. The intense heat and light from the fireball burned shadows of people and objects onto concrete walls—the outline of a man and his handcart, a ladder, a tree. Birds caught fire in midair.

Two miles from the hypocenter, people suffered severe burns. Their clothing was shredded. Patches of skin hung loose from their bodies.

Some looked like creatures from horror movies, their features melted, their faces grotesque. A five-year-old girl reported, "People came fleeing from the nearby streets. One after another they were almost unrecognizable."

To escape the spreading fires, people lowered themselves into Hiroshima's rivers. The waters were soon filled with floating corpses. Some survivors painfully made their way to the safety of the suburbs. As they walked from the city, the stench of burnt bodies filled their nostrils.

Shock waves from the bomb blast also caused injuries and death. A fourth-grade boy told investigators: "When I opened my eyes after being blown at least eight yards, it was as dark as though I had come up against a black-painted fence." Entire neighborhoods were destroyed when houses and stores collapsed in the blast. Many people, trapped in the wreckage, could not be rescued.

Lost were personal documents, photographs, pots and pans, pets, books, clocks, calendars— the stuff of everyday life. Water mains, telephone and electric lines, hospitals, police stations, schools, all lay in ruins. Approximately 48,000 buildings were reduced to rubble, and 76,000 more were damaged. Because it was made of concrete, the shell of the Museum of Science and Industry and its dome remained standing. Later, it became a symbol of the bombing.

*Only a few metal and concrete structures survived the devastating blast of the atomic bomb.*

The atomic bomb showered deadly amounts of radioactive fallout on the city. Radioactive fallout results when particles released in the air from an atomic explosion become attached to dust and fall to the ground. These particles cause harmful changes in the cells of humans and other living things. Thousands of people who survived the initial blast and fires soon fell victim to radiation sickness. Dr. Michihiko Hachiya recorded his patients' symptoms at Hiroshima's Communications Hospital. Their hair was falling out, sores irritated their mouths, and spots appeared on their skin. They suffered vomiting and diarrhea, and their white blood counts were dangerously low. By the end of the year, 140,000 had lost their lives as a result of "Little Boy." Five years later, bomb-related illnesses had claimed 60,000 more victims. For years, people continued developing leukemia and other cancers as a result of the bomb's radioactive fallout.

In 1955, leukemia took the life of twelve-year-old Sadako Sasaki. Like many Japanese, she knew the legend that cranes live for a thousand years. It was believed that making a thousand *origami* paper cranes would cure any sickness. Sadako folded 964 paper cranes before she died. Her saddened classmates completed the task. They continued to fold cranes in memory of other children who had died from the delayed effects of radiation.

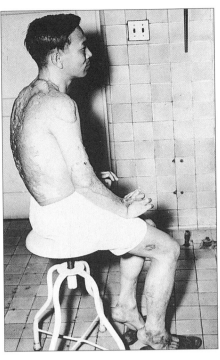

The incredible heat unleashed by the bomb melted this metal clock, held by a Japanese museum worker (left). For decades, survivors developed horrible illnesses from being exposed to the bomb's intense radiation (above).

After the bombing of Hiroshima, the U.S. government announced that it had a terrible new weapon. If Japan did not surrender, it would receive "a rain of ruin from the air, the like of which has never been seen on this earth." The Air Force dropped leaflets over major Japanese cities and broadcast radio messages to the Japanese people. They were told to ask their government to end the war. Otherwise, they would be destroyed like the people of Hiroshima.

Once more, Japanese diplomats appealed to the Soviet Union to help them secure a peace settlement. Despite the bombing, they firmly rejected the demand for unconditional surrender. On August 8, the Soviet Union replied by declaring war on Japan. Joseph Stalin sent troops to seize nearby Manchuria, which Japan had conquered earlier.

According to Truman's July 24 orders, a second atomic bomb would be detonated unless Japan surrendered. Bad weather conditions were forecast for the target cities after August 10, so the bomb had to be dropped immediately. At 3:47 A.M. on August 9, a B-29 bomber named *Bock's Car* left Tinian with "Fat Man" in its bomb bay. This bomb looked like a giant egg with fins. It was more advanced and complicated than "Little Boy." It had to be armed before takeoff, although safety plugs were in place.

*"Fat Man," the bomb dropped on Nagasaki*

Nothing seemed to go right on this mission. The previous night, navy Ensign Bernard J. O'Keefe discovered that a cable had been installed backward during the rush to assemble the bomb. He fixed it. Before takeoff, the pilot, Captain Charles W. Sweeney, learned that a fuel pump on the plane was not working. This meant that there would be no reserve fuel for the return flight. Sweeney decided, "To hell with it. We're going anyway."

Nearly halfway to Japan, a signal light alerted weapons expert Commander Frederick Ashworth that "Fat Man's" safety plugs had failed. For the next half hour, he and his assistant checked the wiring. It turned out to be a false alarm. Then, the camera plane failed to meet up with *Bock's Car* and the instrument plane. The bomber could not call the missing plane by radio because the Japanese would surely hear the message. After a forty-minute search, they had to go on without the camera plane. The delay cost precious fuel.

At 10:44 A.M., the B-29 arrived over the target city of Kokura. *Bock's Car* made three unsuccessful bombing runs because the aiming point, a military arsenal, remained hidden under heavy ground haze and smoke. This gave Japanese fighter planes time to pursue the B-29. Electronics specialist Lieutenant Jacob Beser remembered, "We had some flak bursts

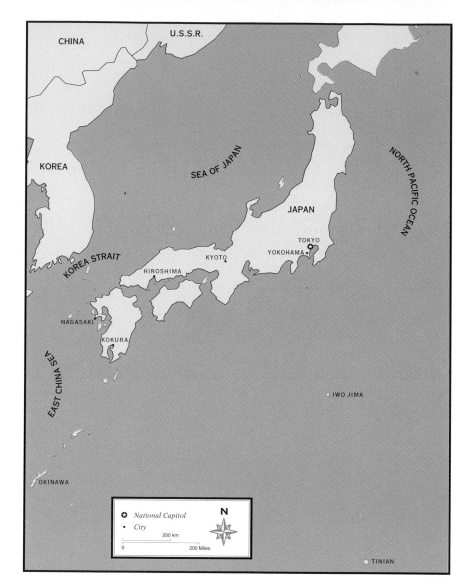

*Bock's Car flew from Tinian Island to Japan to deliver the second atomic bomb. The target city, Kokura, was covered with haze, so the bomber flew up to Nagasaki and dropped the bomb.*

[anti-aircraft fire] and things were getting a little hairy, so Ashworth and Sweeney decided to make a run down to Nagasaki, as there was no sense dragging the bomb home or dropping it in the ocean." The B-29 waggled its wings to alert the instrument plane that it should follow.

The city of Nagasaki was covered with clouds. Captain Sweeney told Commander Ashworth,

"We have enough gas for one pass over Nagasaki. Just one pass…. How about dropping it by radar?" This was in violation of orders. Bombardiers were required to see the targets with their own eyes. Reluctantly, Ashworth agreed with Sweeney. At the last minute, a hole opened in the clouds. Bombardier Kermit Beahan could see a stadium a mile and a half away from the original aiming point, downtown Nagasaki. He released the bomb immediately, yelling, "Bombs away!" Realizing his mistake, he shouted, "Bomb away!" "Fat Man" exploded at 11:02 A.M. with a force equal to 22,000 tons of TNT, nearly twice as powerful as "Little Boy."

*Kermit Beahan*

Captain Sweeney quickly maneuvered the plane away from the city. The mushroom cloud rose and loomed close to the plane. The gunner, Sergeant Ray Gallagher, shouted through the intercom, "Let's get the hell out of here!" Sweeney had less than 300 gallons of gas for the return flight.

A message was radioed to Tinian that *Bock's Car* had completed its mission and would make an emergency landing at Okinawa. On Okinawa, the air control tower did not answer Sweeney's calls. Finally, the bomber's crew shot off flares to attract attention. No one from Tinian had notified the tower that *Bock's Car* would land there. After two hours of refueling, the crew of the B-29 took off for Tinian and arrived safely at 10:25 P.M.

As *Bock's Car* was flying overhead, Governor Nagano of Nagasaki was making plans to help his city survive an atomic bombing. He was too late. Suddenly, "Fat Man" exploded. Nagano saved himself by falling to the ground and rolling away from the intense light. Then he called over one of the few remaining telephone lines for rescuc teams. Within a few hours, they arrived in the city. They were shocked by what they saw.

Most of Nagasaki was on fire. People slowly made their way toward the hills and the nearby bay. Many of them had suffered horrible burns and never reached the outskirts of the city. Half the medical staffs were killed instantly, just when doctors and nurses were needed to treat injuries. The bomb killed 40,000. Another 30,000 died by the end of the year. Over the next five years, bomb-related illnesses claimed 70,000 more lives.

The steep hills around Nagasaki limited the effects of the explosion. Nevertheless, all of the buildings within a thousand acres of the

*Residents of Nagasaki flee the bomb's destruction.*

*More than a month after the bomb was dropped, Nagasaki lay in ruins.*

hypocenter lay in ruins. Eighteen schools were destroyed. The Mitsubishi steel works were crippled, and a huge torpedo factory caught fire. Seven miles from the hypocenter, the windows of many homes were blown out of their frames.

Even after the destruction of Nagasaki, the Japanese government disagreed about surrendering. Most of Japan's military leaders wanted to continue the war. Many civilian officials wanted it to end. To break the deadlock, Emperor Hirohito did an unusual thing. He asked the government leaders "to bear the unbearable" and bring peace to Japan. The emperor was not supposed to involve himself in politics. His was a ceremonial and religious office. The Japanese believed he was divine. Hirohito explained his unexpected interference, saying, "I cannot bear to see my innocent people struggle any longer."

*Japan surrendered on August 14. On September 2, Japanese officials boarded the USS Missouri to sign the official documents that ended the war (right).*

*Emperor Hirohito*

On the same day, August 9, a somber Harry Truman wrote a letter defending his decision to drop the atomic bomb. "Nobody is more disturbed over the use of the Atomic bomb than I am but I was greatly disturbed over the unwarranted attack by the Japanese on Pearl Harbor and their murder of our prisoners of war. The only language they seem to understand is the one we have been using to bombard them." A survey later showed that 75 percent of the American public agreed with Truman's decision to use the bombs.

On the morning of August 10, news that Japan would soon surrender reached Washington, D.C. The Japanese would accept the Potsdam

Declaration but insisted on keeping the emperor as the head of their nation. To end the war, Truman and his advisors prepared a vaguely worded compromise statement. "From the moment of surrender, the authority of the Emperor and the Japanese Government to rule the state shall be subject to the Supreme Commander of the Allied Powers."

On August 14, 1945, the Japanese agreed to surrender. The next day, the Emperor broadcast over the radio to his people. This was the first time they had ever heard his voice. He announced that the war was over because, "The enemy has begun to employ a new and most cruel bomb, the power of which to do damage is indeed incalculable." Japanese officials signed the surrender documents on board the battleship USS *Missouri* on September 2.

Later that month, American and Japanese medical teams began studying the effects of the bombings on the people of Nagasaki and Hiroshima. As the years passed, the effects of the bombings continued to be felt in Japan. Citizens of Hiroshima and Nagasaki faced discrimination by other Japanese. People feared that if they married citizens of Hiroshima or Nagasaki, their children would develop birth defects.

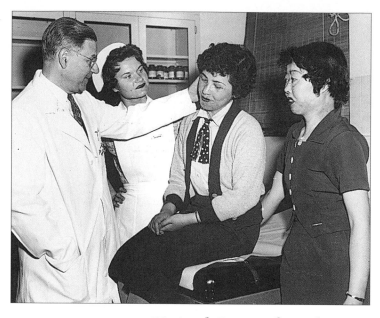

*Two of the Hiroshima Maidens receive medical treatment in New York City in 1955.*

Many of the *hibakusha* (people affected by the atomic bomb) felt guilty about surviving when so many of their loved ones had died. In 1955, one group of *hibakusha,* the Hiroshima Maidens, were brought to the United States for plastic surgery. These women were severely disfigured by the bombing. After she returned home, one woman wrote that the surgery "has made me an entirely new life."

Today, Americans and Japanese are allies and trading partners, but neither nation has completely forgotten the past. Every December 7 at Pearl Harbor, taps is played over the watery grave of the battleship *Arizona,* the final resting place of more than 1,500 men. Americans cast garlands of flowers into the sea to remember those who died in the Japanese air raid. Every August 6, Japanese gather at the Peace Memorial in Hiroshima for a moment of silence. Then they drop lanterns into the Ota River to honor the victims of the atomic bomb. A similar service is held at Nagasaki. Americans and Japanese hope that atomic bombs will never be used again anywhere in the world.

*At the annual Hiroshima and Nagasaki memorial ceremonies, Japanese citizens remember the horror of the atomic bombings and pray that such an event will never be repeated.*

# GLOSSARY

**arsenal** – A building where military weapons are stored; a collection of weapons

*Atomic bomb*

**atomic bomb** – An enormously destructive weapon whose explosive force comes from the energy released by splitting tiny particles of matter, called atoms

**bomb bay** – The section in the body of a plane where a bomb is carried before it is dropped

**bombsight** – A device used to aim bombs at a target

**fireball** – The center of an atomic bomb explosion, which produces intense heat and light

**flak** – Anti-aircraft ammunition fired from fighter planes or from the ground

*hibakusha* – The Japanese word for people affected by the atomic bomb

**hypocenter** – The exact place on the ground over which an atomic bomb is exploded in the air

*origami* – The Japanese art of folding pieces of paper to create colorful shapes or objects

**radar** – A device that bounces radio waves off unseen objects to measure their distance and/or direction

**radiation** – Rays of energy in the form of light and particles that can cause severe burns and harm cells in the body

**shock waves** – Blasts of changing air pressure resulting from an explosion

**unconditional surrender** – The requirement that a defeated nation make no demands on the victor of a war

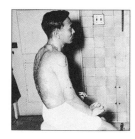

*Burns from radiation*

# TIMELINE

**1939**

*September 1*
Germany invades
Poland; World
War II begins

*September 3*
Great Britain and
France declare
war on Germany

**1940**

*June 10*
Italy joins
Germany,
declares war
on France and
Great Britain

*June 22*
Germany
conquers France

**1941**

**1942** *June 4–6:* Battle of Midway

**1943** *September 3:* Italy surrenders to Allies

**1944** *June 6:* D-Day (Allies land in France)

**1945**

*Pearl Harbor*

*June 22*
Germany invades
Soviet Union

*December 7*
Japan attacks
Pearl Harbor

*December 8*
United States
enters war

*March 16*
Americans capture Iwo Jima

*April 12*
Roosevelt dies; Truman becomes
president

*May 7*
Germany surrenders to Allies;
end of war in Europe

*June 21*
Americans capture Okinawa

*July 16*
Atomic bomb successfully tested

*July 26*
Potsdam Declaration announced

*August 6*
Atomic bombing of Hiroshima

*August 8*
Soviet Union declares war on Japan

*August 9*
Atomic bombing of Nagasaki

*August 14*
Japan agrees to surrender

*September 2*
Japan signs surrender agreement

*Japan surrenders*

## INDEX *(Boldface page numbers indicate illustrations.)*

Aioi Bridge, 6, 16
Ashworth, Frederick, 21, 22–23
atomic bomb, 3–4, **4,** 6, **7,** 10–13, 14, **14,** 16–25
Beahan, Kermit, 23, **23**
Beser, Jacob, 6, 21–22
*Bock's Car,* 20, 21, 23, 24
China, 8, 9
Churchill, Winston, **13**
*Enola Gay,* 3, **3,** 4, 5, 6, 16
"Fat Man," 20, **20,** 21, 23, 24
Ferebee, Thomas, 6
Gallagher, Ray, 23
Germany, 8, 10, 11
Great Britain, 9, 12
Hachiya, Michihiko, 18
*hibakusha,* 28
Hirohito, Emperor, 25, **26,** 27
Hiroshima Maidens, 28, **28**
Hiroshima, Japan, 3, 5, **5,** 6, **7,** 16–18, **18,** 27, 28
Italy, 8
Iwo Jima, 15

Japan, 8–9, 11–12, 13, 15, 16, 20, 25–27
Kokura, Japan, 11, 21
Kyoto, Japan, 11
leukemia, 19
Lewis, Robert, 5
"Little Boy," 4, **4,** 6, 19, 20
Manchuria, 20
Manhattan Project, 10, 12, 14, **14**
maps, 4, 22
Museum of Science and Industry, **1,** 17
Nagano, Governor, 24
Nagasaki, Japan, 11, 22, 23, 24–25, 27, 28
O'Keefe, Bernard, 21
Okinawa, 15, **15,** 23
Ota River, 28
Parsons, Deke, 4, 5
Peace Memorial, 28, **29**
Pearl Harbor, Hawaii, 9, **9,** 13, 26, 28

Philippine Sea, 4
Poland, 8
Potsdam Declaration, 16, 26–27
Potsdam, Germany, 12
Roosevelt, Franklin Delano, 8, **8,** 10, **10**
Sasaki, Sadako, 19
Shima Hospital, 16
Soviet Union, 9, 12, 13, 14, 20
Stalin, Joseph, 13, **13,** 14, 20
Stimson, Henry, 10, **10,** 11
Sweeney, Charles, 21, 22–23
Tibbets, Paul, 3, **3,** 5, 6
Tinian Island, 3, 4, 20, 23
Tokyo, Japan, 15
Truman, Harry S., 8, **8,** 10, 11, 12–13, **13,** 14–16, 20, 26
United States, 8–9, 14
USS *Augusta,* 8
USS *Indianapolis,* 4
USS *Missouri,* **26,** 27
USS *Virginia,* **9**
Van Kirk, Theodore J., 6

## PHOTO CREDITS

Cover, UPI/Bettmann; 1, Reuters/Bettmann; 2, 3, 4 (bottom), AP/Wide World; 5, U.S. Air Force Collection (58446 AC), Courtesy Air and Space Museum, National Smithsonian Institution; 7 (bottom), Bettmann Archive; 7 (top), 8 (both photos), 9, 10, UPI/Bettmann; 13, AP/Wide World; 14, Courtesy Los Alamos National Laboratory; 15, 18, 19 (top), AP/Wide World; 19 (bottom), © Paul Chesley/Tony Stone Images; 20, AP/Wide World; 23, 24, 25, UPI/Bettmann; 26 (all photos), AP/Wide World; 28, UPI/Bettmann; 29 (both photos), © Cameramann International, Ltd.; 30 (both photos), 31 (bottom), AP/Wide World; 31 (left), UPI/Bettmann

## ADDITIONAL PICTURE IDENTIFICATIONS

Cover: *The skeleton frame of Hiroshima's Museum of Science and Industry was one of the only structures to survive the atomic bomb blast.*

Page 1: *Years after the atomic bombing, the shell of the Museum of Science and Industry is the site of the Hiroshima Peace Park. On August 6 every year, a memorial service is held there to remember the bombing of Japan.*

Page 2: *Japanese officials come aboard the USS* Missouri *to sign the surrender documents.*

## EDITORIAL STAFF

Project Editor: Mark Friedman
Design & Electronic Composition: TJS Design
Photo Editor: Jan Izzo
Cornerstones of Freedom Logo: David Cunningham
Original Maps: TJS Design

## ABOUT THE AUTHOR

Barbara Silberdick Feinberg graduated from Wellesley College with honors and went on to earn a Ph.D. in political science from Yale University. This is her fifteenth book on American history and politics for young people. She lives in New York City with her sons, Jeremy and Douglas, and two Yorkshire terriers.